Bless Ye the Lord

Wisdom Tales is an imprint of World Wisdom, Inc.

For my mother.
– F.T.

Library of Congress Cataloging-in-Publication Data

Names: Tyrrell, Frances, illustrator.
Title: Bless ye the Lord : praise song of the three Holy children /
illustrated by Frances Tyrrell.
Other titles: Benedicite, omnia opera Domini. English.
Description: Bloomington : Wisdom Tales, [2023] | Audience: Ages 4-8 |
Audience: Grades 2-3
Identifiers: LCCN 2022026780 (print) | LCCN 2022026781 (ebook) | ISBN
9781937786977 (hardcover) | ISBN 9781937786984 (epub)
Subjects: LCSH: Praise of God--Biblical teaching. | Praise of God--Juvenile
literature. | Nature--Biblical teaching. | Nature--Juvenile literature.
Classification: LCC BS1783 2023 (print) | LCC BS1783 (ebook) | DDC
204/.3--dc23/eng/20220718
LC record available at https://lccn.loc.gov/2022026780
LC ebook record available at https://lccn.loc.gov/2022026781

Printed in China on acid-free paper.

For information address Wisdom Tales,
P.O. Box 2682, Bloomington, Indiana 47402-2682
www.wisdomtalespress.com

Bless Ye the Lord

Praise Song of the Three Holy Children

Illustrated by

Frances Tyrrell

✤Wisdom Tales✤

O all ye Works of the Lord, bless ye the Lord;
Praise him, and magnify him forever.

O ye Angels of the Lord, bless ye the Lord;

Praise him, and magnify him forever.

O ye Heavens, bless ye the Lord;
O ye Waters that be above the
    Firmament, bless ye the Lord;
O ye Powers of the Lord, bless ye
    the Lord;
Praise him, and magnify him forever.

O ye Sun and Moon, bless ye the Lord;
O ye Stars of Heaven, bless ye the Lord;

O ye Showers and Dew, bless ye the Lord;
Praise him, and magnify him forever.

O ye Winds of God, bless ye the Lord;
O ye Fire and Heat, bless ye the Lord;
O ye Winter and Summer,
    bless ye the Lord;
Praise him, and magnify him forever.

O ye Dews and Frosts, bless ye the Lord;
O ye Frost and Cold, bless ye the Lord;

O ye Ice and Snow, bless ye the Lord;
Praise him, and magnify him forever.

O ye Nights and Days, bless ye the Lord;
O ye Light and Darkness, bless ye the Lord;

O ye Lightnings and Clouds, bless ye the Lord;
Praise him, and magnify him forever.

O let the Earth bless the Lord,
O ye Mountains and Hills,
    bless ye the Lord,
O ye green things upon the Earth,
    bless ye the Lord,
Praise him, and magnify him forever.

O ye Wells, bless ye the Lord;
O ye Seas and Floods, bless ye the Lord;
O ye Whales, and all that move in the
    waters, bless ye the Lord;
Praise him, and magnify him forever.

O ye Fowls of the air, bless ye the Lord;
O ye Beasts and Cattle, bless ye the Lord;

O ye Children of men, bless ye the Lord;
Praise him, and magnify him forever.

O let Israel bless the Lord;
O ye Priests of the Lord,
    bless ye the Lord;
O ye Servants of the Lord,
    bless ye the Lord;
Praise him, and magnify him forever.

O ye Spirits and Souls of the Righteous,
bless ye the Lord;

O ye Holy and Humble men of heart,
bless ye the Lord.

O Ananias, Azarias, and Misael,
bless ye the Lord;
Praise him, and magnify him forever.

Amen

Barbary Dove
Streptopelia risoria

BIRDS and BUTTERFLIES
of the Holy Land

Hoopoe
Upupa epops

White Stork
Ciconia ciconia

Great Tit
Parus major

Barn Owl
Tito alba

Bar-headed Goose
Anser indicus

Lesser
Spotted Eagle
Aquila pomarina

Barn Swallow
Hirundo rustica

Eagle Owl
bubo bubo

Tree
Sparrow
Paser montanus

White-Spectacled
Bulbul
Pycnonotus xanthopygos

Rock Dove
Columba livia

White-throated
Kingfisher
Halcyon smyrnensis

Yellow Wagtail
Motacilla flava

Plain Tiger
Danaus chrysippus

Common Blue
Polyommatus icarus

Old World
Swallowtail
Papilio machaon

Turkish Meadow
Brown
Maniola telmessia

Red Admiral
Vanessa atalanta

Painted Lady
Vanessa cardui

BEASTS and CATTLE
of the Holy Land

Lesser Horseshoe Bat
Rhinolophus hipposideros

Caspian Pond Turtle
Mauremys caspica

Steppe Field Mouse
Apodemus witherbyi

Rock Hyrax
Procavia capensis

Golden Squirrel
Sciurus anomalus

Red Fox
Vulpes vulpes

Cape Hare
Lepus capensis

Sheep
Ovis aries

Goat
Capra aegagrus hircus

Lion
Panthera leo

Nubian Ibex
Capra nubiana

Cattle
Bos bos taurus

"Those that move in the waters"

Common Stingray
Dasyatis pastinaca

Sperm Whale
Physeter macrocephalus

Bottlenose Dolphin
Tursiops truncatus

About the Song

Who were the Three Holy Children? Their Hebrew names were Ananias, Azarias, and Misael and their story is in the Book of Daniel. Carefree childhood ended for the three when they and their families were marched away to captivity in far-off Babylon. Years of exile followed. The children grew and were trained to be servants to King Nebuchadnezzar. New names were given to them: Shadrach, Meshach, and Abednego. They were good and trustworthy servants, but they would not bow down to Nebuchadnezzar's golden idol.

"Bow down or be punished!" they were told, but still they refused. The king had them shut into a fiery furnace, hot and terrible. Instead of burning up they were protected by a holy angel who waved the flames away. The three were completely unharmed.

"Shadrach, Meshach, and Abednego, come out!" the king called. He praised their faith and the power of the Lord in protecting them. He gave them and all the captive Hebrews in Babylon permission to worship the Lord freely. The three children gave thanks to the Almighty, who made the world and everything in it, and who saved them in their time of trouble. Their song of praise appears in the Book of Daniel in the oldest versions of the Christian Bible (the Greek Septuagint and Latin Vulgate), and in the Apocrypha of later editions. The abridged version of the song presented here is taken from the *Book of Common Prayer* (1662).

About the Pictures

"Praise Song of the Three Holy Children" calls upon all the creatures of creation to bless, praise, and glorify the Lord. The illustrations show scenes of their childhood days, when Ananias, Azarias, and Misael were free to explore the hills, fields, and streams of their homeland.

The children in the pictures are based on three real children who posed for me. The dog in the book is not a pet, but a working dog that tagged along for the adventure. He does get back to some sheep herding towards the end of the song!

The paintings are watercolors, which is to say, color pigments blended with gum arabic and made to flow by the addition of water. My brushes are soft and flexible: some are "flat" wide brushes and others are "round" with pointed ends, large and small. The paper I use is 100% cotton and is very smooth.

Canaan Dog
Canis lupus familiaris

"Bless ye the Lord"